Love Letters to the Church

God is Longing for His People
to Know Him

Diana Hartling

Library of Congress Control Number: 2003091638
ISBN 1-591606-08-X

Xulon Press
www.XulonPress.com

Xulon Press books are available in bookstores everywhere, and on the Web at www.XulonPress.com.

Dear Esther,

May the Lord continue to bless you as you walk with Him.

Love,

Deana Hartley

Dedications

To God be all the glory! He is the Author and Finisher of all things. May we come to really know Him and His great love for us, and not just know about Him.

And to my beloved husband David, for his love and support for me and endless patience as I struggled to hear from God and be obedient to His call.

Acknowledgements

*T*hank you dear friends, for helping make this book possible and for your love, prayers and support, to be a blessing.

To Leona Cadenhead, the first person I met on the first day of school in seventh grade, and the first person to really encourage me to pursue the call to write the book. To Ed Bacheldor, former church bulletin editor, who took the pages and compiled them into a working manuscript. To Yvonne Davis, for our special prayer times together as I struggled to put the manuscript together.

To Kathleen Brumley, for proofreading and interceding in prayer for the ministry. To Margaret Underwood, for her encouragement and journalistic knowledge in typing up the final draft. And finally, to Marlene Bagnull, prolific author, who after critiquing the manuscript at a Christian writer's conference, encouraged me to pursue getting it published, and not give up.

Table of Contents

Introduction

*M*aybe this is an unusual book because it had an unusual beginning. It all started one night in 1984, as I was driving home from a Bible study in Orlando, Florida. I had been praying for the Lord to give me a ministry, but little did I know He was about to answer my prayer in a most unusual way.

I began to get an urging in my spirit to pull off at the next exit to a shopping mall, and soon my feet were carrying me upstairs to a Christian bookstore on the second level.

"The Lord must have a book He wants me to read," I thought as the Holy Spirit led me down the aisles. Suddenly I stopped, turned to look on the bookshelf, and staring me in the face was a book entitled, *An Introduction to Christian Writing* by Ethel Herr. Instantly I knew that the Lord wanted me to be a writer, but that was not what I wanted to hear.

"No, Lord, I don't know how to write!" I loudly protested, hoping no one would hear as I got in a rather heated argument with God over my inadequacies.

But none of my whining would deter Him, as He quickly responded, "You're right, you don't know how to write; but I do, and I will tell you what to write."

I had no idea what God even wanted me to write, but not long afterward, I began to keep a prayer journal, spend my quiet times listening for the Lord to speak, and jotting down what I felt I heard Him say. Sometimes it was general scriptures from the Bible. On other occasions He might direct me to a verse which would pertain to something He was revealing to me through the Holy Spirit. Some words were specifically for me, but others dealt more with the church as a whole and who we are in Christ.

After two years, the Lord told me to put the material together into a collection for the church, the body of Christ. Little did I know at the time that the release of the book would not be for many years. But as I waited on the Lord, He would send prophesies through others time and again, who didn't know about the manuscript, to let me know it would one day be published. This is that collection.

I believe that the real writer of this book is not flesh and blood, but the Spirit of God who moved on a mortal, a rather reluctant one at that, to write these "Love Letters" to His Beloved Church. Specifically, the Lord told me how much He longed for us to KNOW HIM, not just know about Him. As a bridegroom desires to woo his betrothed to himself, that is how God longs to draw us with cords of love, into that intimate closeness that can only come from knowing Him.

And Jesus not only wants to be the Savior of our soul, but the Lord of our life. He wants to take us from being spiritual children to becoming spiritual giants for God. He wants us to have an intimate relationship with Him, to know His heart. Only out of that union can we then know the Father and the Holy Spirit, and finally grow into maturity. Then we will be able to take our rightful place in the body of Christ and be part of the Army of the Lord, the Church Militant, saving the lost, healing the sick, raising the dead, casting out demons, setting the captives free and taking back what the enemy has stolen.

As you read this prophetic call to action, may you too feel the heartstrings of God drawing you to a closer and more passionate walk with Him. May you hear Him calling you to be part of His end time army and ultimately, His Victorious Church. The time is too short to play games; we must be ready for our Lord's soon return.

Occupy!
Occupy!
Occupy!

Part I
Drawing Near to God

Behold,
I Make All Things New

Behold, I make all things new,
for I am creating a new heaven
and a new earth.
Old things are passed away;
behold, all things have become new!

Don't fret about it;
don't be afraid of it.
It will come as a thief in the night,
as surely as birth pangs come
to a woman in labor.

Behold, I am creating a new heaven
and a new earth!
Old things have become new!

Do not be deceived
by what you see around you.
Or hear in your ears:
business as usual,
people marrying or giving in marriage.

My coming is sure;
I will not hesitate much longer.
My heart grows in longing

to be with My people.
Oh, that everyone would know Me,
repent, and turn from his sin
and be saved!

How I long to heal the nations,
to cover them and heal them
with My precious blood;
but they won't hear
and have become deaf to My cry.
They won't listen to Me anymore.
Their heads are full of their own words;
they can't hear Me anymore.

Pray that their ears would be opened
before it is too late.
Pray that they would seek Me
with their whole heart.

You listen to my voice:
I won't leave you in confusion;
I'll be there when you need Me;
I won't let you down.

Scripture References:

    Revelation 21:1-5
    I Thessalonians 5:1-3
    Matthew 24:37-39
    Acts 3:19
    Matthew 13:14-15
    Jeremiah 31:33-34
    Deuteronomy 7:9

Abide in Me

Abide in Me.
My Spirit is upon you,
for I have created you
and made you whole.

If you seek Me, you will find Me,
if you seek Me with your whole heart.
And, if you ask,
it shall be given to you,
if you ask in faith, believing.

I won't let you down;
I won't disappoint you,
but you must abide in Me
and let My words abide in you,
that you might know Me
and My desire for you.

I hunger for your love
even as you hunger for Mine.
Don't let the things of the world
get in the way of our relationship.
I have much to say, but not now;
you need to be grounded in My love,
so that it will be like breathing,
for I am closer than hands or feet.

My Spirit seeks to abide
in you continually,
not off and on
like an electrical switch.

Don't depend on feelings alone
to know My presence,
or the enemy will come in
and try to distract you
and seek to take My word
out of your heart,
before it can even take root.

I am with you always,
don't be afraid;
for when you do reach out by faith,
then you will begin to bring forth
much fruit to My glory.

Scripture References:

John 15:4-11
Deuteronomy 4:29
Matthew 7:7
Mark 11:23-24
James 1:2-8
Matthew 13:19-23

I Am Your Foundation

I am your Foundation
and your Rock.
And when the storms come
and the winds blow,
your house will not fall
if it is grounded in Me.

I am your Support
and the Cornerstone
the builders rejected.
Lean on Me,
hold on tight,
I won't let you down.

Rest in My arms;
lean back and receive
My Peace,
My Joy,
My Love,
for I am sturdy and sure
and will not be moved.

Scripture References:

> Luke 6:47-48
> I Peter 1:6-8
> Isaiah 28:16
> Galatians 5:22-23

My Sheep Know My Voice

I love you and My Father loves you.
Allow the Holy Spirit to come in
that He may take up residence in your soul,
that your joy may be full,
and that you may no longer be tossed
to and fro by every wind of doctrine.

People speak for Me all the time,
but they are not Me.
Some faithfully interpret My words
and some only seek to take advantage
of My love for My people.
And so you need My Spirit
abiding in you continually,
that you may know the truth.

I am the Truth; and the Spirit of Truth,
the Holy Spirit bears witness of Me.
Abide in Me and let My words abide in you.

I will bless you,
but you must listen to My voice.
You must know My voice;
My sheep know My voice.

Do not be deceived by those in authority,
by men who say they are speaking for Me.

I want you to know the truth;
I want you to know Me.

Scripture References:

I John 1:4
Ezekiel 3:17-21
John 15:7
John 16:13-15
Ephesians 4: 11-16
John 10:27
John 14:6

Listen to My Voice

Listen to My voice
and do not let My words
depart from your lips,
for they are true
and there is no darkness in them.

You are so afraid of being hurt
and of being deceived
that you have built up a shell
around yourself.

I can break that shell
if you will let Me.
If you will abide in Me
and let My words abide in you,
then you won't be afraid
of misinterpreting Me.

You won't be afraid
that it might be the voice
of the enemy,
instead of the voice
of your God and King.

See My hands;
See My feet;
thrust your hand into My side.
Blessed are those who have not seen
and yet have believed.
Pray that you, too, may believe
without having to see.

For if you walk by faith,
you will not be made blind;
for then you will see and hear things
men have longed to see and hear,
but have neither seen nor heard.

Remember that a child
does not start out running.
First, he must begin to crawl,
then to stand, then walk,
and finally, he is able to run,.

Don't get frustrated,
for I am there every inch of the way,
taking you by the hand,
helping you along bit by bit,
as much as you are able
to handle at a time.
So let My faith grow up in you,
and you'll be amazed
how your love has grown too.

Scripture References:

    Proverbs 4:20-22
    John 15:7
    John 20:26-29
    Matthew 13:13-17
    Philippians 1:6
    Hebrews 6:1-2
    I Corinthians 13

I Want You to Know Me

My will and My desire for My people
are that they would know Me,
not just about Me,
but really know Me.
How can they say, "We know God,"
when they never listen
for Me to speak to them?

If you knew Me,
you would obey Me
and you would love Me.
And why would you do these things?
Because you knew My heart.

My love has not grown cold
nor have I changed;
but the hearts of men
have grown cold and hard.
They seek to glorify themselves
rather than their God.

All day long I stretch out My hands
to a perverse generation.
Awake, oh dreamer, from your sleep!
Arise and wash your face,
for the Son of Man shall soon return

with healing in His wings.

For if you shall turn from your sin,
and ask for My forgiveness,
and believe in Me,
you shall be saved.

But to him who will not listen,
it shall be a day of judgment,
of gloom and doom and thick darkness
on the face of the earth.

Remember, I have called you
out of darkness into light.
Walk in My light,
for in Me there is no darkness at all.

Scripture References:

    Jeremiah 31:33-34
    John 15:10
    Ezekiel 11:19-20
    Isaiah 65:2
    Ephesians 5:14
    Romans 10:8-10
    Zephaniah 1:14-16
    I Peter 2:9-10

Ask Me and I Will Tell You

I am the Lord your God
and I will not be stomped
under the feet of men!

I cry out,
but will anyone listen to My plea?
Does anyone want to know how I feel?
Does anyone stop to ask Me?
If you want to know something,
ask Me and I will tell you.

Too many people are running around
saying, "God said 'this,' or 'that.'"
If it were I who was speaking to them,
would they not all be in agreement,
instead of fighting among themselves?

I am not a divided God.
My ways are clear to all
who will listen to Me.
If you ask, I will tell you.
I don't play games with My children.

Remember to test the spirits,
and not to believe every spirit,
no matter how seducing or convincing

it may sound.
My words burn like a fire
in the hearts of My people.
I am not a wishy-washy God!

Scripture References:

James 1:5
I Corinthians 12
Jeremiah 23:25-32
Matthew 7:7-8
I John 4:1-6
Luke 24:32

Don't Be Afraid I

Is there anything impossible for Me?
Then why won't you believe?
Why won't you let Me overcome your fear?

You say that you want to please Me,
to glorify My name.
To do that, you must be willing
to step out in faith.

Remember when I walked out on the Sea of
Galilee?
Peter asked if he might join Me;
and I bid him to come.

As he stepped out of the boat
and upon the water by faith,
he did fine as long as his eyes were on Me,
but as soon as he began to look around
and see the waves and feel the winds,
he became fearful.

Doubt said, "This is impossible;
people can't do things like that!"
Fear soon replaced faith,
and he began to sink.

But looking up, he cried out to Me
and I reached out My hand,
grabbed him and held him up.

I was there for Peter,
and I will be there for you too,
but you must be willing to
stick your feet over the side
of your boat and let go,
even in the midst of a storm.

I know it's hard to do;
I was also tempted in every way,
just like you.

I know what you are going through.
You're afraid people will laugh at you;
they laughed at Me.

You're afraid that you have nothing to give;
yet you have asked the Father for gifts
and He has given them to you.
Use them to bring glory to God,
don't keep them to yourself.

The sheep know the voice of their shepherd,
and you know Mine, "I am with you always,
and I will never leave you or forsake you."

Did I let Peter down?
Did I let him drown?
No, and I won't let you, either;

but you must learn to trust Me.

And how do you do that?
By surrendering to God,
submitting yourself to the Father,
even as I have submitted Myself to Him.

Don't be afraid,
for the Father loves you,
even as I love you
and gave Myself for you.
Abide in that love
and don't be afraid.

Scripture References:

Jeremiah 32:27
James 1:5-8
Matthew 14:22-33
Hebrews 4:15-16
I Corinthians. 10:13
I Corinthians 12
John 10:2-4
Matthew 28:19-20
John 3:16-17
John 16:25-27

Don't Be Afraid II

Don't doubt in your heart
what I have spoken to you.
Don't be double-minded
in word or deed, but believing.

Don't be afraid to speak the truth
for fear of being condemned,
but come into the light
that those thoughts in your heart
may be brought before Me.

Don't be afraid to come to Me.
As a child needs to come to his father,
so you need to come to Me and ask,
if you have any questions.

I don't want you to be afraid
that I will condemn you;
but if you seek to hide from Me,
know that there is nothing
hidden that shall not be revealed,
for I already know your heart.

My word is true,
and there is no darkness in it at all.
I want you to learn to trust Me

in all things,
not just the ones you are sure of
in your heart.

I will faithfully watch over My children
in all their ways.
I will not suffer your foot to be moved
nor your foundation to be taken away,
for I am your foundation and your God.

Scripture References:

James 1:6-8
Matthew 7:7-11
Proverbs 3:5-7
I Corinthians 3:11
Romans 8:1-5
Luke 12:2-3
Psalm 121

Children of the Light

Walk as children of light,
not of darkness,
but discerning darkness from light,
and light from darkness.

Rest all of your confidence
on Me alone,
not on yourself,
living after the flesh
and the appetites thereof.

But you are the children of the Light;
and so walk in that Light,
knowing that I am that Light
in which you walk
when you abide in Me.

Scripture References:

John 12:35-36
Ephesians 5:1-14
John 1:1-5

You Must Choose

It is My desire to feed
and nourish My people
so that they will flourish.

I want them to know Me,
not just about Me,
but to know Me for themselves.
Then their hearts won't be confused;
then they won't be used as pawns
in the hands of the enemy.

I have come that you might have life,
and have it more abundantly.
Won't you abide in Me
and let Me abide in you?
Submit to God.
Resist the devil
and he will flee from you.
He seeks only to sow seeds
of doubt and fear within your heart,
that you might be in bondage to him.

But I have set you free!
I have cut off the bonds that held you!
So keep your eyes on Me.
Don't let go.
Don't turn to the right or to the left,

nor let things distract you from My love.

I'm right here.
I'm not going anywhere;
you can depend on Me.
I am your Lord and your God;
I love you with an undying love.
None can separate you from My presence,
but you must choose whom you will serve.

I won't stand in line;
I must be first in your life
or not at all.
You must choose.
I won't forsake you;
I seek only to build you up,
to give you safety in My arms.

Remember the relationship
between a husband and his wife,
between a bridegroom and his bride—
so must be the relationship
between Christ and His church,
for I want you to be without
spot or wrinkle.

I will cover you with My mantle;
I will protect you and stand up
for you before My Father.
And because you are covered by My blood,
you are now washed clean by it also.
I have laid down My life for My bride.

Scripture References:

> Hebrews 8:10-12
> John 10:10
> John 15:7
> James 4:7
> Psalm 139:7-12
> Ephesians 5:25-30
> Isaiah 30:21
> John 8:36
> Joshua 24:14 -15
> I John 1:6-7

Suffer the Little Children

"Suffer the little children to come unto Me,
and forbid them not;
for of such is the kingdom of God."

How I long to reach out to them,
but the fear of not being received by Me
and the fear of their elders
has kept us apart.
If only they will come to Me,
I will take away their fear and doubt.

Those who would try to keep them from Me,
don't know Me or My love for My children.
If they knew Me,
they would love Me and My Father,
who sent Me;
but as it is, they neither know Me nor My Father,

Scripture References:

Mark 10:13-15
Matthew 18:1-6
Matthew 23:13
John 8:17-19

I Am All You Need

I have come to build up,
not destroy My people,
that they may be a blessing
in My sight.

Trust Me for all of your needs—
spiritual, emotional, and physical.
There is no need to worry about tomorrow;
it is in My hands.

I am He, who calmed the raging sea,
Who set the captives free,
Who raised the dead to life,
Who healed the paralytic,
the blind, deaf and dumb.
Is there anything too hard for Me?
No, there is not, nor ever will be!

If you have Me,
you have all that you could possibly want
or even imagine.
I love you with all My heart,
even more than you could possibly believe.

I am your heavenly Father,
your Lord and Savior,
the Holy Spirit.

I am who I am—
there is no other!

I will cradle you in My arms
and protect you
like a mighty fortress.
The enemy shall not prevail
for his power is limited,
but Mine is unlimited!

Seek My protection until
the storm has passed,
for I will hide you
in the cleft of the rock.
Under My shadow
you will find safety,
and I will cover you with
My wings.

Scripture References:

Jeremiah 29:11
II Corinthians 9:8
Acts 10:38
John 17:1-3
II Peter 1:10-11
Acts 1:8
Exodus 3:13-15
Psalm 91:1-4

Remember Who Your Lord and Master Is

Your ways are not My ways,
but draw near to Me
and I will draw near to you.

Seek Me while I may be found,
even as a precious stone
or a gem of great worth.
For My words are life and health
to those who find them.

Let them become an integral
part of your being,
as essential as food and water,
for they are heavenly nourishment
and profit both body and soul.

Remember who your Lord and Master is.
Let not your heart be troubled,
neither let it be afraid;
but let Me have full reign in your life.

Remember who it is that you serve,
that the servant is not greater
than his master.
It is enough that he be as his master.
You are My servant.

Scripture References:

Isaiah 55:6-9
Matthew 13:45-46
Proverbs 4:20-22
John 14:27
Matthew 10:24-25

Be Strong and of Good Courage

Be strong and of good courage,
and I will lift you up,
out of your pit of despair.

Fear not,
for I am with you to uphold you
with My victorious right hand.

Fret not yourself over evil doers,
for I have put all things under My feet.
And if you follow Me,
then you are seated with Me
in heavenly places,
and all these things
shall be under your feet also.

So, fear not, I say!
For My kingdom comes in glory
and power over things past,
over things present, and over things to come!

Reach out and touch
your brother and sister
with My love,
even as I have reached out
and touched you

with My love and My Father's love.

Fear not, I say,
for if your hope is in Me,
you shall not be disappointed
or brought to shame.
I will lift you up;
I will give you hope.

Prayer:

Your words are true, Oh Lord, and there is no darkness in them at all. For they are light in the midst of darkness and hope in time of despair. One word from Your lips can fell the mightiest army or greatest kingdom, for there is no other God besides You. All glory, honor, and power be Yours forever. In Jesus' name I pray. Amen.

Scripture References:

Joshua 1:7-9
Psalm 40:1-2
Isaiah 41:10-13
Ephesians 2:4-7
John 15:12-13
Romans 5:5

Part II
Growing Into Maturity

Call to Prayer

Beware of men who speak of peace
for the sake of peace.
For there will be no peace
until My return;
but chaos and turmoil,
anxiety and fear will reign
in the world.

My people, who are called by My name
need to pray and build up
a mighty fortress of prayer warriors—
a battlement impenetrable to the enemy.

Then they shall march as one body
with one mind, fully armed
with the protection of My armor,
lifting My banner high;
slaying dragons by the power of My word,
bringing down strongholds,
and setting the captives free.
Then the liberated ones -
freed from the enemy's grasp -
shall join with them marching under My command.

In Me there is victory,
and you will find it in no other.
Though one search the world over

there is only darkness and defeat
to those who don't know Me,
for they are still in bondage
and are slaves to Satan and to the desires and lusts
of the flesh.

Be careful for nothing,
but remember, in all things to pray;
for the time will come when they
will no longer listen to sound doctrine,
but with itching ears they will seek out those
who will satisfy their lustful desires.

A time of great darkness is coming upon this world
and only those who hear My voice and obey it
will know which way to turn;
for My word shall be your light and lamp,
and your prayers will ignite the match
that makes it burn.

Therefore, keep your lamps lit,
so you won't be wandering around in the dark
with the rest of the world.

Scripture References:

I Thessalonians 5:1-11
Ephesians 6:10-20
Deuteronomy 4:35
II Timothy 4:2-4
Psalm 119:105

II Chronicles 7:14
II Corinthians 10:3-6
Philippians 4:6-7
I John 2:15-17
Matthew 25:1-13

I Am the Good Shepherd

I will put My word within you;
do not fear.
I am your Redeemer and Shepherd.
I know how to keep My sheep from harm,
even My little ones.

I will put My love in your heart
and you will wonder,
"When was it, when that love wasn't there?"
For it will be as though
you had never been without it.

I will touch your body
and you shall be made whole,
for I already took away your infirmities
when I died on the cross.

Don't forget what has been done for you,
be aware of it always.
Man cannot save himself;
only God can save!

Wake up and hear My words,
For I am about to rattle cages
In the higher echelons of society,
And give hope to those
Who put their trust in Me.

You shall have peace
while the world has war;
you shall rejoice and be glad
while the world weeps and mourns;
you shall have total serenity
of mind, body and spirit
while the world is full of chaos
and losing its mind.

I won't take My hand off you
to leave you when you need me most!
I'll be there!
Fear not, little flock,
for I am the Good Shepherd,
who lays down His life for the sheep.

Scripture References:

John 10:11-16
I Peter 2:24-25
Psalm 44
Luke 6:20-28
I John 4:7-16
Hebrews 7:25
John 14:27
Hebrews 13:5

I Have Come to Set the Captives Free

Hear My voice;
cling to My every word.
I have come to heal,
not to destroy,
to deliver and save,
not to tear down and imprison;
to set the captives free.

I want them to know My love,
which is poured out for them
by My blood.
My love is pure
and my words are true;
there is help and hope
in no other.

Let the dying cry out to Me
before it's too late;
let the servant and his master
come to Me.
Don't hesitate:
the time is near,
closer than before.

With tears I cry out
to these My people,

who are called by my name:
"Speak out to the lost;
don't be silent.
Their time is running out!"

Trust Me to speak through you.
You have trusted Me for your salvation,
won't you now trust Me for theirs?

You may bring My word to them,
but remember,
they must decide whom they will follow;
you can't make the decision for them.

You will have accomplished
that which I have commanded,
if you do what I have said.
Be true and faithful to My word
and I will lift you up
and give you My hope.

Prayer:

Lord, help me to speak out Your word in faith,
trusting you for each word, each sentence, each idea.
Help me also to speak in love, showing forth Your
compassion to the people, that they may see You in
me and glorify You. All this I ask in Jesus' mighty
and holy Name. Amen.

Scripture References:

> Jeremiah 24:6-7
> Luke 19:10
> Isaiah 53
> Luke 4:14-19
> Mark 16:15-16
> Acts 16:31
> Ezekiel 3:17-21
> John 10:10
> Heb. 12:1-3

I Am the Light

While you have the Light,
use it to shed light in the darkness.
I am the Light,
and he who has Me and is abiding in Me
has the Light and is full of light,
and that light will not go out
as long as he remains in Me.

The world is in spiritual darkness;
it doesn't see the light
or even know the Light exists.
But when those in that darkness
come to the Light, the devil must flee.
He cannot stand to be exposed
to the Light.

For the Light burns away their sin
and the lonely separation is gone.
They have gained new life;
old things have passed away;
all things have become new.
The scales on their eyes have fallen off,
and now they can really see Me.

Scripture References:

John 12:35-36
John 8:12
John 3:19-21
Revelation 21:5

Draw Near to Me

Draw near to Me
and I will draw near to you.
Seek Me and you will find Me,
if you seek Me with all your heart.
Abide in Me and let My words
abide in you.

The world is always running
after a new trend,
but they don't see the One
who can change their hearts.

They want so much to be accepted,
but know nothing of Him
who desires to accept them,
who desires for them to know Him
and become His children.
I, the Lord, can change their hearts
as easily as they change their garments.
Nothing is too hard for me – nothing.

Scripture References:

James 4:8
Jeremiah 29:13
John 15:7

John 17:14-26
Mark 8:34-37
Romans 8:14-21
Ezekiel 36:25-27
Jeremiah 32:27

Let Not Your Heart Be Troubled

I will not leave you
with a burdened mind
or a fearful heart,
for I have come to redeem,
not destroy.

Let not your heart be troubled;
neither let it be afraid.
I am your hope and your confidence.
Put your trust in Me alone.

I am with you,
so don't be afraid
or let the enemy trick you
into believing a lie.
Look to Me, not to circumstances.
Remember when the children of Israel
were trapped between Pharaoh's army
and the Red Sea?
It was I who divided the waters
and carried them across as on dry land.
In quietness and confidence,
you shall find your strength.

Scripture References:

    Hebrews 13:5
    John 14:27
    Proverbs 3:25-26
    John 8:44
    Exodus 14:9-31
    Isaiah 30:15

I Will Bless My People

I will bless My people
with My enduring love.
I will pour out rivers of living water
from their bellies, without measure.
My Spirit will flow to all
who will receive Me.

I know your frame,
that you are but dust.
I know how much of My Spirit
you can stand,
but someday there will be
no holding back.

In the twinkling of an eye
you shall no longer be flesh and blood,
but shall have a new body,
an immortal body, incorruptible;
and then you shall behold Me as I am,
in all My glory and righteousness.

My love is stronger than death,
and nothing shall be able
to separate Me from My children,
My little ones, My people again.

Scripture References:

John 7:37-39
I Corinthians 13:9-12
I Corinthians 15:42-58
Romans 8:35-39

Oaks of Righteousness

I shall bless you
and you shall be blessed.
I shall establish you
and you shall be established.

You shall be as a tree
planted by the waters,
whose roots grow deep down
into the soil.

You shall not be rooted up
or torn down,
but shall be like a great oak,
shading and protecting
those under your care.

You shall spread out your branches
in all directions,
and many shall find rest
and refreshment under your boughs.

Because you have established
yourself in Me
and allowed the seed of My word
to grow in your heart,

I will bless you
and your inheritance
shall be established.

Scripture References:

Genesis 12:2
Psalm 1:1-3
Jeremiah 17:7-8
Jeremiah 29:11
Mark 4:14-20
Psalm 37:18-19
Acts 20:32

You Are No Longer Unclean

I have taken your fear away
and covered your sins with My blood.
You are no longer unclean in My sight
or in My Father's sight.

Now you are clean -
white as snow -
without spot or blemish,
and you are Mine.

I jealously guard over My children
like jewels of the highest order,
that no thief may break in
and steal them away.
None can pluck them out of My hand.

The only way the enemy can get a foothold,
is through the door of their heart.
If they let him in,
he will set up shop
and again they will be in bondage.

But I will not lie down and watch
My people perish;
I will fight for them like a whirlwind
across the desert.

You, too, must pray
and intercede for them,
that they may be delivered
from unbelieving hearts and minds.

I am painting pictures for them,
if they will only receive what I am saying,
"Protect your heart and so guard your salvation."

Scripture References:

Psalm 32:1-2
Isaiah 1:18
Zechariah 9:14-16
John 10:27-30
II Chronicles 7:14
I John 1:9
Ephesians 5:24-27
I Peter 2:4-5
James 1:13-15
Proverbs 4:20-23

Pray for the Peace of Jerusalem

Pray for the peace of Jerusalem
>   and for those who seek to destroy
>   My people Israel, My firstborn;
>   she in whom My soul delights.

>   For in the last days
>   there will be great devastation.
>   The enemy knows his time is short,
>   and he will seek to destroy all traces
of My people from the face of the earth.
But I will lift up a standard against him,
>   and he shall not prevail.

>   Guard your mind and your thoughts;
>   test the spirits and continually seek Me,
>   even for small things.
Stay in such constant communication with Me,
>   that you won't be taken in when the enemy
>   comes to you in sheep's clothing.

>   Beneath his disguise, is a roaring lion
>   seeking whom he may devour,
so grab hold of your faith with both hands,
>   and don't let go!

Don't be deceived by those who try
to convince you that My words aren't true
or seek to tell you there is another way.
Don't listen to them!

For through your faith, your soul is saved from
death;
I can't stress this enough.

Too many who call themselves Christians
have tried for too long to be a friend
to God and the world at the same time.
This must not be,
lest you be sucked into thinking as the world thinks,
doing as the world does
and becoming an enemy to God Himself.
The time has come to choose sides;
choose whom you will serve.
"As for me and my house, we will serve the Lord!"

Scripture References:

Psalm 122:6-9
Jeremiah 31:9
Malachi 4:1-3
Isaiah 59:19
I John 4:1-6
I Peter 5:8-10
Galatians 1:6-9
Hebrews 10:35-39

I John 2:15-29
Joshua 24:15

PART III
Becoming the Church Militant

My Kingdom

I have given you authority in My Name.
Use it!
Don't let yourself become double-minded,
unsure of what you believe to be true.

For the enemy knows if he can attack
a kingdom from within and get the people
to doubt and be confused about those
in authority,
then that kingdom will become divided,
and like a blind man having no direction.
It will surely fall.

But if that kingdom knows the King,
and has given allegiance to Him,
and honors His word,
then that kingdom cannot be divided.

There will be no room for the enemy
to sneak in the door and upset the people.
There will be no place for him to hide
or carry out his plans to sabotage
the kingdom.

The people will be of one mind,
one heart, one will,
and nothing will be able to penetrate

that barrier of faith.
That kingdom will stand,
for it cannot and will not be divided.

Scripture References:

John 14:12-14
James 1:5-8
Mark 3:24-25
John 17
Daniel 7:13-14

His Plan

The devil will try to come to you
with everything he can throw at you -
but don't accept it.
He will try to put fear, worry,
and doubt in your heart -
but don't receive them.

And all these things he will do,
in order to hurt Me.
Remember that it is jealousy that
got him in trouble in the first place.

He hates Me and wants the throne
I share with My Father.
He hates His creation,
especially the church,
because it represents Me,
to a world lost in sin.

Yes, he thinks he can destroy My love
for My people, My little ones, My own.
But he is wrong!
No weapon formed against them
shall prosper!

He is already a defeated foe!
Defeated by My precious blood,

defeated at Calvary two thousand years ago. No, not even the gates of hell shall prevail against My church.

Scripture References:

Isaiah 59:19
II Timothy 1:6-14
Isaiah 14:12-17
Revelation. 12:7-17
Isaiah 54:17
Matthew 16:15-18

Call to Arms

There is power in My Name,
as in no other.
There was none before Me
and there will be none after Me.

Pray for the unity of My people,
that they would no longer be
like a house divided against itself,
backbiting, tearing its walls down
from within.

I am your Captain,
the Commander of Armies,
the King of Kings.
I give My commands
and nations rise or fall;
they are like clay in My hands.

Are the very soldiers in My regiment
so busy fighting among themselves
that they can not even see that
the enemy is at their borders -
and even now is approaching from
outside the city walls?

Where are My watchers on the walls?
Have they also joined in the debate,

instead of listening to My voice
calling them to arms?

My people perish for lack of knowledge
But what kind of knowledge are they receiving?
My prophets are too busy telling everyone
why they should be listening to their
opinion of the world situation,
and why it should be discussed at length,
instead of calling My people to prayer.

Awake, O sleeper, and warn the people!
Sound the alarm!
Stop your dancing and merrymaking.
Prepare a fast, weep and mourn.
Seek My face before it's too late.
Hear My people! Be on the lookout!

Pay attention to the words of My mouth!
For the enemy is trying a last ditch effort
to deceive, if it were possible, even the elect,
all who are called by My name,
both Israel and those outside the gates,
who are My flock, even those who have received
Me.

Scripture References:

Isaiah 44:6-8
Matthew 12:25
Heb. 2:10

Joshua 5:13-15
Revelation 17:14
Ezekiel 3:17-19
Hosea 4:6
Ephesians 5:14-21
Joel 2:15-17
Rev. 12:10-12
Matthew 24:23-24
John 10:16

My Army, My Church

I am building My people up,
My army, My church.
Look around you
and you can see Me at work.

Do you see it?
Do you hear it?
My army is marching,
fully equipped,
to declare My word
to a world lost in sin.
They're getting louder!
They're getting organized
by My Spirit!

My word is being sent forth
LOUD AND CLEAR!
But all too often it is falling
on deaf ears,
and eyes clouded
by the worldliness around them.

My army is a praying army,
made up of intercessors
crying out to Me for the lost,
the sick, those in prison
and those who are alone.

My army is valiant in battle,
lifting up My word as a sword,
defeating the enemy, blow for blow.

My army hears clearly My every word
and doesn't hesitate to act.
My army is ever rejoicing
and glorifying My Name.

Scripture References:

Ephesians 6:12-17
Mark 4:9-20
I Thessalonians 5:16-18
I Tim 2:1-6
Hebrews 4:12

Looking for Signs

∞

Everyone is looking for SIGNS,
they look here, they look there.
They read My Word like a text book
or a puzzle map,
trying to be the first to come up
with the answer to the question,
"When will Jesus return?"

I'm tired of it!
Stop looking for signs and look to Me,
the Author and Finisher of your faith!

They say, "We want Jesus to come back soon,"
but they don't know what they are asking.
Are they really ready for Me to come back?
Don't they realize, it's My earnest desire
that no one perish?
Are they still without understanding?

I have stayed away waiting, agonizing,
putting off coming back
until the last possible moment,
so that as many people might be saved
as possible.

It is with tears that I write this,
because I long with deep groanings

to be with My people,
and they with Me, together forever,
with nothing separating us again.

Because of the Father's great love for creation,
He has not given Me the go-ahead to return.
There is still time,
but it is running out.

So Church, don't seek after signs,
but rather occupy until I come.
Spend your time telling others about Me,
not watching the sky.

When I return, everyone will know it's Me,
from the east to the west,
from the north to the south,
but then it will be too late to tell them
about My love and salvation.

Don't be deceived by the enemy.
Occupy!
Occupy!
Occupy!

Scripture References:

II Peter 3:3-14
Hebrews 12:2
James 4:3-5
Romans 8:14-27

John 3:16-17
Matthew 24:4-44

Are You Ready?

Let not your heart be troubled,
neither let it be afraid of the days ahead.
For persecution will come to all
who seek to live godly lives.

Creation shall wax worse and worse
as the coming of the Lord approaches.
The love of many will grow cold,
but if you endure until the end,
you shall be saved (delivered).

Don't be anxious about anything,
but pray about everything,
making your requests known
to God with thanksgiving.
Then His peace shall keep your heart
and mind through Christ Jesus.

Pray without ceasing,
preach the word,
be diligent in season
and out of season;
reprove, rebuke, and exhort
with patience and the word of God.

For the time will come when they
will not endure sound doctrine,

but will follow their own lusts,
and turn from the truth to fables.

But be not afraid of them,
for greater is He that is in you,
than he that is in the world.
Yes, be of good cheer,
I have overcome the world.

Scripture References:

John 14:27
Matthew 24:3-14
Philippians 4:6-7
I Thessalonians 5:17
II Timothy 3:12-17
II Timothy 4:2-4
I John 4:4
John 16:33

More Than a Conqueror

Hold My banner high,
wear your armor well;
tread down the enemy,
that serpent,
beneath your feet.
He is already a defeated foe.

Don't give place to the devil
by fighting with your bare fists.
Your battle is not with flesh and blood,
but against principalities and powers
in heavenly places.
The weapons of your warfare are not carnal,
but mighty through God to the pulling down
of strongholds.

By my precious blood,
the word of your testimony,
and by not loving your life unto death,
you shall overcome him
and be made more than a conqueror
through Me because I love you
and gave Myself for you.

Scripture References:

Ephesians 6:10-18
II Corinthians 10:3-6
Revelation 12:10-11
Romans 8: 37-39
Ephesians 5:25

I Go Before You

I am the shade upon your right hand
and shall bring you from the darkness
into My glorious Light.
I am the Life-Giver.
What I give no one can take away
nor pluck out of My hand.

I am your Deliverer and Counselor,
Arm yourself for battle,
for I go before you.
Rest in My strength;
I will defend you.

Keep all your armor on,
and the shield of faith held high,
that you may not be hit
by a stray arrow.
For Satan's forces seek,
not only to stop you,
but to destroy your very soul.

But do not fear.
Greater is He that is in you
than he that is in the world.

I am Jehovah;
I am your God,

and I Am is fighting with a mighty fury
for My People, the church,
but they must fight too,
and not stop until My return,
for My ministers shall be as flames of fire,
speaking forth My word,
for the perfecting of the saints
for the work of the ministry,
for the edifying of the body of Christ,
till all come to the unity of the faith
and the knowledge of the Son of God,
into a perfect man,
into the maturity and fullness of Christ.

Then the church will no longer be as children,
tossed about by every wind of doctrine;
but rather, will have grown up in Christ,
who is the head of the body,
even the church.

Scripture References:

Psalm 121:5-6
John 1:4
John 10:25-30
Psalm 34:7
John 14:15-17
Ephesians 6:11-18
I John 4:4
Ephesians 4:11-15

Pray For My People, the Church

Pray for My people, the church
concerning the persecutions
that lie ahead,
that they may be strong and persevere.

I am so pleased that they
want to really know Me,
for I so desire for them
to know My love for them;
and they can,
if they will continue
to reach out to Me and to
their brothers and sisters in Christ.

The world is hungry,
starving to know Me,
and they don't even know it.
They are like babies with no teeth,
who can't digest much at a time
or else it all comes up undigested
on everyone.
What a mess!

I have planted My words
in the hearts of My people.
Like small seeds,

these words will germinate and grow
with the right attention.
The correct spiritual food, water
and Sonlight shed on these small plants
can work miracles to bring forth
a huge harvest of souls.

You are My people, My planting.
Don't be afraid to grow up
and mature in Me,
for I only desire good things
for My children.

As you mature,
you will really learn
how to be a witness to the world
that has only heard of Me,
but doesn't know Me;
nor can they know Me without
the Spirit of God bearing witness
to their spirit as to who I am.

If you do not have the light of Christ,
the Holy Spirit burning inside you,
how will the world be able
to see the Light,
and so come out of the darkness
and into the Light?

That is why you need to be filled
with My Spirit on a daily basis,
not just now and then when you think of it -

or on special occasions
when you are asked to pray;
but be continually filled with the Spirit
and do not be afraid.

So, let your Light shine before men,
that they may see your good works
and glorify your Father who is in heaven.

Scripture References:

Matthew 24:1-44
Hebrews 12:1-3
Matthew 5:6
Philippians 2:2-7
I Peter 6:1-2
Matthew 13:3-23
Isaiah 61:3
Hebrews 6:1
Luke 11:33-36
Romans 8: 26-27
John 3:19-21
John 7:37-39
Ephesians 5:18
Matt.5:15-16

Forget Not My People, Israel

Forget not My people, Israel,
who are called My people,
and are called by My name.
They need My constant protection
from the enemy,
for he has vowed to destroy them
until there is not one left alive
in all the earth.

But My hand of mercy is outstretched,
and I have put a buffer between them
and their enemies;
yet they need to know that it is I,
the Lord, who is preserving them,
and not the power of their own hands.

They must not become puffed up
with self pride,
but give credit where credit is due,
for I am a jealous God and will not be mocked,
nor give My glory to another.

Pray that their spiritual eyes
will be opened to see Me as I am,
and realize how much I have loved them;
then the veil will be lifted
and they will be grafted back

into the True Vine.
And all My people everywhere
will be one people,
one flock, with one Shepherd.

Scripture References:

Genesis 12:1-3
Genesis 35:10-12
Jeremiah 31:31-34
John 10:7-11
Deuteronomy 4:33-40
Psalm 44:1-8
Ezekiel 36:16-32
Ezekiel 39:22-29
II Corinthians 3:13-18
Isaiah 52:13-15
Isaiah 53
Romans 11
John 10:14-18

God's Protective Love

I have loved you with an everlasting love.
With bowels of mercies poured out,
so have I loved My children,
My little ones, My own.

Fear not, for I am with you,
and I will protect you.
With My right hand I will defend you
from your enemies,
and with My left hand I will cradle you
under My arm and close to My breast.
You need not fear, for I will be
your Protector and Champion.

I am your Heavenly Father
and I love you very much.
Grow in My love for you,
through what My Son has already done,
for He has given all.
He has held back nothing from Me,
that He might give you everything.

Scripture References:

Jeremiah 31:3
Luke 13:34

Romans 8:32
Psalm 17:7-9
Psalm 121

Watch and Pray

I have heard the prayers of My people
calling out to Me,
pleading and weeping before Me.

I have heard, and I will perform
My will through My power,
and not by the power of mere man.
I will be lifted up!
I will be glorified!
My people will not be put to shame!

If My people weep, I weep more;
if they cry out in their hurt
at what they see,
do I not cry out even more?

My will shall be done!
I do not lag behind,
as others would suggest or have you believe.
I know everything that is going on,
but you cannot see the whole picture
nor the battles in the heavenlies.

I say unto you, "Hold on, do not waver;
You shall not be put to shame,
if you put your trust in Me."
I am coming soon!

Cease not your prayers
for those who know Me not.

As things heat up, and they will,
perhaps then they will turn to Me
before it is too late,
before there is no time left
and no way out.

Forget not, you are in the battle too.
Continue to build up yourself in My Word,
in the power of My Name,
and by My Blood that was shed for you.
In it is great power!

Be single-minded, looking straight ahead,
not to the left or to the right.
Be filled with the Holy Ghost daily,
and repent and turn from your sins
whenever you fall away, even for a moment.

Remember, the enemy knows his time is short
and he will do whatever he can to stop
God's people from performing
what the Lord has called them to do.

Don't let the enemy come in
through the door of your home,
and even on your property.
Don't let him get to you through
your family, friends, or neighbors,
not even those with whom you work.

Don't give the enemy a foothold
in your life!

Keep your eyes on Me and you won't fall.
I will guide you and keep you
from slipping.
I love you; remain in My love.
For if you love Me, you will obey Me.
Trust Me to help you to obey
My every word.

The time is too short to play games,
the enemy is just over the rise,
and My soon return is imminent.
Don't be as the foolish virgins were
when the bridegroom appeared,
fast asleep and out of oil.

Watch and pray that you may not
enter into temptation.
What I say, I say unto all,
"Watch and pray."

Scripture References:

Jeremiah 31:1-26
Zechariah 4:6
Isaiah 54:4-5
II Peter 3:8-15
Ephesians 6:12
Hebrews 10:23

Ephesians 5:18
Revelation 12:11-12
John 10:10
Psalm 94:16-18
John 14:23-24
Matthew 25:1-13
Matthew 26:41

A Victorious Church

My people, My church,
My body here on earth,
is getting ready to turn
the world upside down!
It won't be long!

Yes, My church will be victorious
in the tearing down of strongholds.
The devil is on the run,
and they have become a roaring lion;
they're mad!

Their eyes have been opened
and they now realize that they
had been deceived by the enemy
all of their lives,
but no more!

The weakest of them will be
stronger than an army,
and the strongest of them
greater than a legion of armies.

I shall return to a victorious church,
one that has been busy
setting the captives free,
healing the sick,

casting out demons,
raising the dead,
and telling the Good News to a lost generation
that has become both deaf and blind.

My coming is sure.
With each new day, it draws closer than before.
Will they be ready?

Scripture References:

Ephesians 1:18-23
Acts 17:6-7
II Corinthians 10:3-5
Titus 3:3-7
Hebrews 2:14-18
Leviticus 26:7-12
Matthew 10:7-8
Matthew 24:1-44

Some Final Thoughts

∽

*J*ames 4:8 says, "Draw nigh to God, and he will draw nigh to you." And in Romans 10:13 we find, "Whosoever shall call upon the name of the Lord shall be saved."

God is calling His people to Himself in these last days. All, who out of a humble and repentant heart, will call upon the name of Jesus Christ, shall be saved.

If by reading this book, it has made you hungry to know the love of God in a deeper way, won't you take a few minutes right now to say this prayer:

Dear Lord, I thank You that You really love me and want a personal and intimate relationship with me. I too want to know you better, and the Bible says the only way to come to the Father is through your Son, Jesus Christ.

Lord Jesus, thank You for dying on the cross for me and shedding Your blood for my sins. I confess to You that I am a sinner and ask that You would forgive me and cleanse me from every sin. Please come into my life and be my Lord and Savior. Fill me with the Holy Spirit and use me for Your glory, for I long to really know You, not just know about You. In Jesus' name. Amen.

If you are already a Christian, but long to draw closer to God, begin today to seek the Lord for Himself, not just for what He can do for you. He will restore the joy of your salvation when your heart's desire is for Him alone.

Pray with me:

Dear Lord, I realize that I have become dry and want the Fountain of Living Water to well up within me. Touch me now by Your Spirit and fill me up to overflowing. Be more real to me than ever before and restore the joy of my salvation. For in Your presence is "fullness of joy," and at Your right hand there are "pleasures for evermore." In Jesus' name I pray. Amen.